S0-CCF-468

To

From

Little Christmas Treasures

The Traditions of Christmas

By Claudine Gandolfi

Illustrated by Jenny Faw

Peter Pauper Press, Inc.
WHITE PLAINS, NEW YORK

This book is dedicated to my family, friends, and the child in us all.

Book design by Arlene Greco

Copyright © 1997
Peter Pauper Press, Inc.
202 Mamaroneck Avenue
White Plains, NY 10601
All rights reserved
ISBN 0-88088-818-0
Printed in China
7

Visit us at www.peterpauper.com

Contents

Introduction

Christmas—the mention of the word is enough to inspire anyone to thoughts of peace on earth, celebrations with family and friends, Santa, and, of course, presents under the tree. But where and how did our current traditions originate? On the following pages you will find the roots of and variations on a host of

our Christmas customs, as well as favorite holiday films. As you'll see, many traditions have been passed down from generation to generation, yet some of our current practices are startlingly recent. We hope this book encourages you to invent some of your own family traditions, and we wish you a wonder-filled holiday.

C. G.

Christmas Firsts

The concept of the Christmas Tree was brought to us by the Germans, who decorated the first tree in Strasbourg in 1605. The practice quickly spread to Switzerland and Austria. In the early 1800s the Scandinavians and Russians began putting up trees, and Parisians finally caught the fever in 1840.

J. C. Horsley designed the first
Christmas card in 1843. This
Victorian invention simply said
"A Merry Christmas and a Happy
New Year to you."

The first reusable ornaments
were created in the 1870s.
Before that, the tree was usually
decorated with candles and edible
foods. It was a real treat to take
down the tree on the Epiphany!

The tradition of the Yule log
originated in Ancient Persia (Iran)
where a wheel or *Yole* was cut
from a very old tree. This wheel
was divided into four sections
to be burned during the four
seasons, the last being burned
at Christmastime.

Washington Irving's *History of New York from the Beginning of the World to the End of the Dutch Dynasty* (1809), described St. Nick as both legend and truth. Irving was the first to costume him as a sturdy Dutchman with a pipe, who rode a wagon full of gifts over the rooftops.

It was in 1821 that Santa first rode his now famous sleigh, which was bestowed on him by an anonymous poet who was also the first to associate reindeer with Santa.

Clement Clarke Moore wrote his famous *A Visit From St. Nicholas* for his children, in 1822. While he borrowed heavily from Washington Irving's image of Santa, Moore was the first to call Santa "chubby and plump." Before that, St. Nicholas was always a thin, older gentleman. Moore was also the first to attribute eight reindeer to Santa, and to name them.

The earliest recorded celebration
of Advent was in 581. In 600
Pope Gregory I decreed that the
fourth Sunday before Christmas
should be fixed as the first day
of Advent. This season is a
preparation for Christmas,
and for the second coming
of Christ.

The word Christmas is derived from Christ's Mass and was first used in 1038. Many holidays during this time were named after saints (e.g., Michaelmas).

Poinsettia was first used as a
Christmas decoration by a
Mexican priest in Taxco.

Silver tinsel garland was introduced as a tree adornment in 1878. Glass ornaments originated in Lauscha, Germany.

The first appearance of Mrs. Claus was in 1889, when Katharine Lee Bates wrote *Goody Santa Claus on a Sleigh Ride*. Ms. Bates later wrote *America the Beautiful*.

German born illustrator Thomas Nast was the first to give us a glimpse of our modern day Santa. Nast also added Santa's Naughty & Nice list, as well as his North Pole workshop.

The first Christmas bonus was given by the Lorillard tobacco company in Jersey City. They surprised employees with a bonus of one week's salary.

The most famous reindeer of all, Rudolph, was the creation of Robert May, a copywriter for Montgomery Ward. In 1939 the company needed a giveaway for department store Santas to distribute. May quickly wrote *Rudolph, The Red-Nosed Reindeer* to go with the stuffed toys. It was later recorded by Gene Autry and has become a holiday favorite.

Prince Albert, husband to Queen Victoria, and being of Germanic descent, introduced the German idea of the Christmas Tree to England in 1841.

In 1923, President Calvin Coolidge established the tradition of the National Christmas Tree for the United States. It was decorated and put up on the White House lawn, as it has been every year since.

Traditions from Around the World

Czechs and Poles cut a branch from a cherry tree. If the branch blooms indoors, it is a sign of good luck in the coming year, and also signifies a short winter.

British children write letters to Father Christmas, just as American children write to Santa Claus. However, in Great Britain they don't mail these letters, but rather throw them in the fireplace and burn them. British children believe that Father Christmas reads their wishes on the smoke from the chimney.

In Poland, the *Wigilia* is a 24-hour fast followed by a 12-course meal, which is observed on Christmas. Participants may eat only after the first star of the evening has revealed itself. In this manner the guiding star of Bethlehem is remembered. Christmas is often called *Gwiazdka*, or "little star," as well as the traditional *Bozz Narodzenie*.

The Christmas stocking originated in Great Britain. According to legend, Father Christmas dropped some gold coins while coming down the chimney. The coins would have been lost if someone hadn't put their stockings out to dry over the fireplace! Children loyally display their stockings on the mantelpiece just in case Santa drops one of his gifts again.

In Sweden, the feast of St. Lucia (December 13) officially marks the beginning of the Christmas season. The saint appears dressed all in white with a crown of candles, and brings saffron buns called *Lussekatter.*

In the French town of d'Auris
Station, people gather to celebrate
Christmas Eve by skiing down a
mountainside with lit torches.
This beautiful custom is said to
bring on an early spring.

Mexicans celebrate the *posada* on December 16. They reenact the Holy Family's trek for shelter. For nine days children go from door to door futilely begging for a safe haven.

On December 26 the British celebrate Boxing Day. Customarily, boxes were put out for donations to the poor and for "tips" for servants and public workers.

The Swedish have a custom called *Julkapp*, which sounds like something from April Fool's Day. Someone is chosen to knock on doors and throw a gift into homes. This gift is part treat and part trick for it has many layers. The more wrapping taken off, the more successful the *Julkapp*.

Rev. John Pitard's hymn *Sancte Claus* popularized St. Nicholas during the American Revolution, and this led to confusion between the saint's feast day, December 5, and Christmas, December 25.

Saint Nicholas, the patron saint
of Russia, was originally a bishop
of Myra in Asia Minor (Turkey),
and is associated with many
miracles concerning gift-giving
and children. In the Middle Ages
presents were given on his feast
day, December 6.

In Greece, the *Skarkántzalos*, or Christ log, is burned for the twelve days of Christmas to prevent the *Kalikántzari* (goblins) from entering the house and performing mischief.

The Yule log has a long history. The proper tradition, from England, states that the log should be from a very old tree to assure sufficient width. Each person who helps to bring in the log is assured of prosperity for the coming year. As you can imagine, this led to large gatherings!

To properly light a Yule log one must use a scrap left over from last year's log. The French traditionally douse the log with a glass of wine for luck. A Yule log must burn for the 12 days between Christmas and the Epiphany, which is why large logs work best.

Celluloid Christmas Favorites

A Christmas Carol (1951 with Alastair Sim, 1984 with George C. Scott) Charles Dickens' classic tale of Scrooge's redemption.

A Christmas Story (1983) Hilarious 40s Americana piece on kid who wants a BB gun.

Holiday Inn (1942) Bing Crosby and Fred Astaire in a love triangle at an inn during Christmas.

Home Alone (1990) Comedy about a child (Macaulay Culkin) who is accidentally left home while his family goes to Europe for Christmas.

It's A Wonderful Life (1946) The ultimate Christmas tale, starring James Stewart and Donna Reed, shows how each life is connected to others.

Miracle on 34th Street (1947 with Natalie Wood, 1994 with Mara Wilson) Kind old gentleman thinks he's Santa and is taken to court.

Santa Claus—The Movie (1985) Comedy on how Santa came to be.

Scrooged (1988) Bill Murray does Dickens' tale with a modern edge.

The Bishop's Wife (1947) Cary Grant in a classic about an angel who helps David Niven build a church and pay attention to his wife, played by Loretta Young.

The Christmas Box (1995) Maureen O'Hara takes in a contemporary couple and teaches them the true meaning of Christmas.

The Preacher's Wife (1996) Retelling of *The Bishop's Wife* with Denzel Washington and Whitney Houston.

The Santa Clause (1994) A suburban father, played by Tim Allen, becomes Santa due to a little known clause.

White Christmas (1954) Bing Crosby and Danny Kaye, while performing their act in an old country inn, each finds romance.

Floral Expressions of the Holidays

According to English custom, for each kiss received under the mistletoe a berry had to be removed. Once all berries were removed, the kissing was complete and prosperity reigned.

British lore tells that a woman who is not kissed while standing under mistletoe will not be married during the coming year.

Chinese Christians decorate their trees with paper lanterns, paper flowers, and paper chains. They refer to these trees as "trees of light."

In India mango and banana trees are used in place of evergreens as Christmas trees. The leaves of the mango tree are also used to decorate houses.

Early Celts and the Ainu of Japan were among the first to believe in the magical properties of mistletoe. Kissing, associated with mistletoe, is probably a remnant of the kiss of peace that greeted visitors as a welcome in medieval times.

Holly is used as a symbol of the
crown of thorns that Jesus wore
during the passion.

Poinsettias require at least 14 hours of darkness each day for 2 1/2 months in order to produce the red leaves associated with the holidays. The actual bloom of the flower is the yellow center.

The French use the *hellebore* flower during Christmas. The legend of the "Christmas Rose" tells of a young bell-ringer of Rouen named Nicaise whose soul was saved from damnation by the miracle of these flowers blooming in the snow.

In Italy and many other European
countries a *ceppo,* or a multi-tiered,
wooden triangle, was used in place
of a Christmas tree. It was traditionally decorated with colored
paper, cones, and candles. The
presèpio or Nativity was placed
at the lower tier.

Unusual Christmas Facts

"Good" King Wenceslaus was the Duke of Bohemia. He made peace with the German King Henry I (Fowler) in the 10th century. It is said that many centuries later, while fighting in Bohemia, British troops heard the song and brought it back home with them.

Christmas was the day preferred by monarchs for coronation in the Middle Ages. Many, including Charlemagne (800), and William the Conqueror (1066) were crowned on Christmas.

George Washington crossed the
Delaware River on Christmas
night, 1776 and won the battles
of Trenton and Princeton.

Drinking Eggnog during Christmas was a colonial invention. The name of the drink is probably a corruption of Egg 'n Grog, which was the colloquial name for rum.

During a battle in World War I a truce was declared between the Germans and the British. This Christmas truce, initiated by the Germans, was marked by caroling. Each side joined in and a true, albeit temporary, cessation of hostilities was enjoyed for the day.

During the 13th and 14th centuries caroling became popular in Europe. The singing of simple and joyous tales was often accompanied by festive dancing.

In the ruins of Glastonbury Abbey, in Somerset, England, stands a thorn shrub that blooms only on Christmas. It is said that Joseph of Arimathea, upon arriving in England, struck his staff on that spot and the shrub grew. Some say it represents Christ's crown of thorns.

Norwegians send a Christmas tree to the English every year as thanks for their assistance in World War II. It is decorated and displayed for all to see in London's Trafalgar Square.

It is in Matthew's version of the gospel that the Three Wise Men or Magi make their appearance. It is said they were following a star to Bethlehem to pay homage to the newborn king.

According to legend, the venerated King Arthur received the sword Excalibur on Christmas.

Many Russians found a way around the Communist ban on Christmas by trimming their "New Year's" tree!

Mumming or *guising*, dressing up in outrageous costumes and making merry in the streets, was a popular Medieval Christmas pastime. Later on, the time was switched from Christmas to the period before Lent. Today we know these celebrations as Carnivale and Mardi Gras (Fat Tuesday).

Frankincense is a gum resin that contains volatile oil, which emits a strong aroma when burned. Its source is an Oriental tree that is found in northeastern Africa and Arabia.

Myrrh is a gum resin of aromatic properties that comes from trees grown in Africa and Arabia. Its taste is bitter and it ranges in color from yellowish brown to reddish brown. It was highly valued in ancient times and used as an additive in perfume and incense.

Norwegians purify their homes for Christmas by attaching bundles of oats and wheat to a long pole and chasing out the evil spirits.

The feast of the Epiphany (January 6) commemorates the first divulgence of Jesus to the Gentiles.

Oliver Cromwell's Puritan
Council outlawed Christmas on
December 22, 1657, and prohibit-
ed dining on mince pie and plum
porridge. Massachusetts and
Connecticut colonies followed suit
in 1659, while Virginia remained
loyal to the Christmas tradition.

Prince Vladimir, an 11th century Russian Prince, traveled to Constantinople to be baptized. On his journey he heard many tales of the miraculous Saint Nicholas. When he returned, he introduced this version of Santa to the Russian people.

The Magi were kings representing Europe, Africa, and the Middle East and arrived bearing gifts of gold, frankincense, and myrrh. They were first identified as Balthasar, Melchior, and Caspar (Gaspar) in a mosaic located in Ravenna, Italy, from the 6th century.

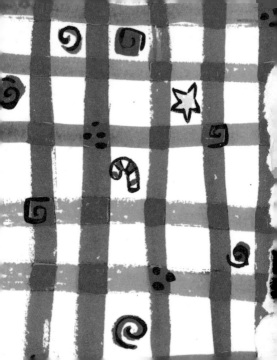